Dark *Night* of the *Soul*

A Story of Ascension

By Poetess
Domonique Tirah Smith

Dedication

To Niko, Na'Imah and Achilles

When everything goes dark, it's you who brings
me back to me.

I

Table of Contents

"The *Dark Night of the Soul* is a spiritual depression, a kind of existential crisis, that requires a deep and painful dip that must be experienced before enlightenment."

Goodbye Ego.

Preface

First and foremost, I must thank Spirit for blessing me with the ability to paint this picture of my journey with my words. Let me take this opportunity to tell you how this collection came about. I was honorably discharged from the United States Navy in 2016. I spent the first two years of my service in a combat zone and my latter years protecting essential government assets. I faced several traumas while in service, one of them being a sexual assault. As a result, I was diagnosed with PTSD in 2018, after experiencing episodes of psychosis related to my traumas.

My transition from sailor to civilian wasn't as easy as I had anticipated and being a single mother didn't make it any easier. I maintained for a while and then I found myself homeless with my, then, three-year-old son. This was the hardest time of my life. Having never experienced much financial hardship, hitting rock bottom was devastating. Though I couldn't see it at the time, this truly turned out to be such a beautiful humbling experience for me. I reached out to several veteran organizations who helped me to get on my feet. This taught me that it's okay to accept help from outside sources. All the while, I still battled depression and anxiety on and off and because of my episodes, I began therapy. It took me two years to open up and get comfortable speaking with my therapist about the things that I faced.

These experiences brought about an involuntary obsession with personal development and that is when my spiritual journey began, and my Dark Night of the Soul commenced. I began to connect with nature and appreciate the beauty of the small things that money couldn't buy. When you have nothing, it either forces you to become bitter or to appreciate the things that you do have. I experienced a deep sense of gratitude. I was able to see that no matter how little I had, Spirit always provided for my needs and the more gratitude I displayed, genuinely, the more blessings I received. When I realized that everything is connected, I understood that I was never truly alone. I came to peace, knowing that the different forces of nature are merely different manifestations of God and I could connect with that source through anything that made sense to me. I also realized that what makes sense to me might not make sense to another, and it's because of that, that I began to respect anyone's truth that might differ from my own beliefs. One can't get to this point without first getting tested and going through a period of darkness, that to most might seem suffocating and paralyzing. There is a light at the end of the tunnel and traveling through the dark will make you appreciate the light so much more. One must get to know their lower self and bring it into balance with their higher self. This is when extensive reflection takes place, called shadow work and essentially the main purpose of a Dark Night of the Soul.

Through all of this, I can't leave out a major focal point of this story. The catalyst that sparked the drive for me to write. While dealing with all this emotional baggage from my past, I was involved in an abusive relationship. Not abusive in a physical sense, but in an emotionally unfulfilling type of way. We parted ways with neither of us knowing how the other truly felt, but I was able to reflect and release all my hidden emotions through these poems. This relationship ultimately helped me grow emotionally because as a result I got comfortable with solitude. It catapulted me into a darkness that I could only get through by transforming. I began to enjoy those quiet moments in the depths of my mind that allowed me to observe myself from a different point of view. I began to look at my relationship to self from an observer perspective as opposed to the observed. I accepted the negative aspects as well as the positive, which allowed self-love to grow and flourish within me. My flaws are just as beautiful as my strengths and without both, I can't be me.

Ultimately, I was able to walk away fulfilling myself emotionally, with a new defined sense of purpose.

It was during my period of hospitalization that I began to write this book. I took my traumas and picked them apart. I was faced with triggers that forced me to dive deep within to heal. I had to accept the fact that I wasn't a victim of the things I faced and some of the experiences I had were passed down through generations to ultimately be healed by me. I'm a warrior and a survivor, and I must use my story to help uplift others who have been in similar situations or going through them. The more I suppressed and ignored my emotions, the more I held myself back and stunted my growth spiritually. I learned that to heal, I must first feel and then release. These experiences were all a part of my ascension.

In my quiet moments and with the synchronicities that I was blessed with from Spirit, my view of the world changed. My empathic abilities left me feeling like the weight of the world was on my shoulders. Recognizing that everyone has a voice, and the way we use that voice can either heal or destroy, I chose to use mine to spread love. I choose to use mine to let others know that they can grow from adversity. I choose mine to speak on things that others are afraid to. And I choose mine to show that we can't move forward until we first work on ourselves. I pray that by reading this collection you can get a deeper sense of who I am, how I've grown and hopefully it will help those going through their

Dark Night of the Soul or dealing with depression and anxiety. Remember to have faith, pray in whatever way makes sense, spread love and always believe in yourself.

The Shadows

The Rooms

Prisoners held hostage,
by hostages themselves.
Only the hostages that hold the prisoners
don't know that they need help.
Observed and contained by those who need
a diagnosis too, but society paints the picture that
their credentials
uphold their truths.
Questions! Questions!
They ask this.
Want to know that.
Their eyes tell a story.
Its empathy they lack.
Unintentional judgments soon become the norm.
Then they shove medicine down the throats of
those
who just need an ear and guidance to get them
through
their storms.
Show them that you're angry,
they'll lock you in a room.
Suppress and medicate!
You're forced to conquer your own gloom.
Can you do it alone?
Can your mind handle that much reflection?
Will you encounter happiness on your plight of
introspection?

Or will the thralls of your thoughts lead you to
inner insurrection?

Whatever the outcome,
it's best, to self, stay true.
Realize that there's a path and plan that's
specially designed for you.
Overcome those nasty voices.
They only want you to remain blue;
And when the road gets too hazy,
know that love and faith will lead you through.

Ego Trip

Sometimes I love when my ego comes out to play;
A soliloquy of my most boisterous behavior.
Sensuality slivers through my pores,
ejecting pheromones as sweet as nectar.
I can glide across a room;
body moving as graceful as an angel's wings.
Sheathed in elegance and in my prime;
The epitome of heaven on earth.

Then I begin to regress.
As I let traumas of my past cast shadows
that would haunt me.
I dove headfirst back into the mundane,
grasping for a sense of validation that I didn't need.
I let negativity permeate my thoughts.
I became my own worst enemy.

Fluorescently Twisted

A soul can choose to be good and choose to be
    wicked, but what
do you do with a soul that fluorescently twisted?
What do you do with a soul that's lazily
    enthusiastic?
A soul that's wickedly depressed
A soul that's brightly fantastic—
What do you do with such a soul?
A soul that shimmies away from evil;
A soul that welcomes in the good—
A soul that's lined with too much compassion;
A soul that doesn't cry as often as it should—
What do you do with a soul so beautifully ugly?
A soul that spreads so much light to others
    but in return receives the lack;
A soul that's magnificently damaged;
A soul that accepts the lashes on its back—
What do you do with a soul that's so selfishly
    selfless?
A soul that clings to a habitual darkness;
A soul that searches for resonating vibrations,
still lost within the twilight,
but handles it with such sophistication—
What do you do with such a soul?
Can someone point it in the right direction?
A soul so meritoriously glorious;
A soul in desperate need of correction.
Has anyone seen such a soul?
Just tell me it can Still

be Brilliant.
A soul that's unappreciative, yet so
Thankful.
A soul that's so peacefully militant.

Is there a heaven or a hell for this soul?
Or somewhere in between?
Does such a soul deserve to be loved?
Does it deserve a shoulder, to lean?

Please!
Can someone tell me?
Is there anyone who will listen?
What do we do with a beautiful
soul that just happens to
be
fluorescently twisted?

Initiation

Sometimes I fill the space that used to be filled with
you
      with optimism and unrealistic dreams.
I stretch my hands to the sky,
      begging for an answer.
Only to be left with my prayers unheard.
Have you left me?
Can you not see the hot,
      liquid emotions rolling down my cheeks?
A sinner by nature;
I feel remorse,
      -but still I continue.
Will you intervene on this self-destructive path I've
chosen?
Who is this person?
Am I an imitation of this world?
Pulling away from temptation,
the world draws me back in with a snarl.
Will you intervene?
Head barely above the surface;
I am drowning in this life
and
      No One can see.
I paint a smile upon my lips and stand tall to create
the illusion.
I am fine.
I lie to myself.
I am fine.
I lie to them,

-but I cannot lie to you.
Will you intervene?
Will you save me from this monster I've created?
A phony.
A fraud.
Praised by onlookers,
        -but it is me who has deceived.
I am not fine.
            S l o w l y
crumbling away.
Will you intervene?
Save me from this world.
Save me from me.

Consciousness

Where do you go when the weight of the world
becomes too much to bear?
When you can barely keep your head above the
surface?
Where do you go when you are the light,
surrounded by so much darkness?
Shining bright for all the world to see;
Vulnerability exploiting all flaws and insecurities.
Where do you go when your blue skies turn to gray?
When everything you touch withers, dies and fades
away?
Where do you go when you can no longer take the
agony of painting that smile upon your face?
Where do you go when in a room full of silence, the
voices become too much to bear?
When the sound of your breath leaves you
trembling in fear?
When the reflection in the mirror is unfamiliar and

d i s t o r t e d;

Where do you go?

Heart at sea

I was a rose,
      on a black sand beach;
Dragged away by a current so coarse.
All my petals were scattered and lost at sea.
All that remained were my thorns;
Meant to be ugly symbols of the pains I've had to
endure.
Pricks of disappointment, betrayal, and
hopelessness pushed my petals through the darkest
waves of sorrow.
Torn by salt that ripped through flesh,
my petals endured torture, pain and harrow.
Somehow they ended washed up on an unfamiliar
shore.
Isolated and alone,
      my petals began to dry and shrivel.
They've come too far from home.
The winds,
      they carried them through brushes that left
only withered pieces of what once was vibrant
flesh-

Oblivion

Who told yesterday she could bring her pain into
tomorrow?
Who told her that she could bring her sorrows into
today?
The heartache she brought shocked my soul into
oblivion;
An emptiness that nothing could abate.
Sunken into a state of regression.
All my healing gone awry.
An abyss of never-ending torment,
and still,
no tears would fall from my eyes.

I let the pain fester.
With time I began to feel numb.
My days became as grim as a withered tree.
All I longed for was the sun.

Why did she whisk my heart into seclusion?
Why did she trigger my anxiety?
Why did she bombard me with these delusions?

Twilight

When your heart gets lonely,
        where do you go?
Do you travel to the depths of your soul?
Who do you call when the wickedness of the
world
        is too much for your soul to bear?
When your dreams are your only escape from
reality?
Then your dreams become your reality.
The people you meet;
The places you go.
Your subconscious becomes your
consciousness.
Are you just merely a confused soul,
        unaware of your surroundings?
Unable to differentiate spirit, physical and
emotional.
Who will save you from this confusion?
Can you can save yourself?

Love

Illogically Yours

I looked into your eyes and saw something colder than ice.
The type of chill that turns bones into dust,
        but I didn't rush to safety because in my eyes,
my light would protect me from your darkness.
The mere fact of knowing that I needed protection
should have been enough to send me on my way, but
I ignored the chills that were sent down my spine
with every thought of you.
I ignored the itch that had begun to develop
        with every moment you were away.
Not realizing that I had become an addict,
        you became my drug of choice
        and only you controlled my doses.
Some would say I was a prisoner,
                but tell me,
        what type of captive enjoys being held by
their captor?
Some dark twisted individual I would imagine.
You see the type of love I had developed was no
fairytale or the type that you see in the movies.
There were no butterflies fluttering in my stomach
or everlasting laughter.
I had turned my high expectations and fear of the
unknown into peace.
I took a step back from logic and disassociated the
connection between mind and heart.
What's the point in logic when all it ever does is tell
me that you're no good?
Logic took one look at you and threw you away.

It was logic that drew my attention to your inconsistencies and broken promises.

It was logic that provoked me to examine you under a microscope.

There, was where my disassociation began.

I saw the pain, anger, fear, regret, disappointments and frustrations.

I felt them just the same.

I saw wounds that had healed improperly.

I felt a darkness
       that could have only grown so big from being cultivated for so long.

Logic told me to run.

It questioned how one could love something so damaged.

For a moment, I did run.

I saged every hole, crack and crevice of my life trying to rid myself of your spirit.

I doused myself in vinegar.

I drank the water from a temple, in hopes that it would cleanse me from within.

I kept my lights on for months and combatted demons while the world slept.

Logic was ready to turn you into a carcass;

Only to be eaten by vultures.

It was my heart that saved you.

You see, through the eyes of my heart, all of the ugliness that makes you, "you", is Beautiful.

3

We've been through lifetimes together.
We've transcended and ascended through time.
Bonding and thickening our cords,
to ultimately come into one this lifetime.
There are no do-overs.
No second tries.
The universe prepared us.
You can see it in her signs.
Put through tests of our faith,
to get us perfectly aligned,
and complete the trinity of you, me and the
Divine.
To step into our purpose,
                    alone
we must thrive.
Learn how to love ourselves first,
so that we can spread peace and light,
and let unconditional love be the driver of our
lives.
Alone we do damage,
but together, we're a force.
Fulfilling our sacred contract,
and nothing can throw us off course.

Love Flame

We started as friends,
then soon became lovers.
We experienced a comfortability so great
between
      each other.
I became the nurturer of your soul,
      but that made you shy away.
You thought it was too good to be true
      and sabotaged our love.
Yet, still I stayed.
We planted seeds in each other's hearts.
Always a part of a bigger plan.
We shot love arrows in the air with hopes that
on
      each other
is where they'd land.
Lucky for us,
our spirits proved it true.
Bonded by love;
You had me and I, you.

Thoughts of You

Thoughts of you bring warmth;
Like sun rays blissfully penetrating my smooth
brown skin.
Thoughts of you bring turbulence;
Like tidal waves crashing down.
Thoughts of you bring tranquility;
Like watching a bumblebee suck the nectar out
of a delicate flower.
Thoughts of you bring darkness;
Like a sky with no moon or stars in the middle
of the Mediterranean.
Thoughts of you bring bubbly happiness;
Like the smile of a child running through
puddles on a cool autumn afternoon.
Thoughts of you bring confusion;
Like a lost cub in the middle of the wilderness.
Thoughts of you bring joy;
Like the first sight of a newborn.
Thoughts of you bring pain;
Like the longing of a heart in solitude.
Thoughts of you make me dizzy.
How I wish I could escape these thoughts of
you.

SOS

I dreamt of white horses galloping towards the
sunset.
You were there waiting by the waters of the sea.
I dreamt of pink sand beaches and massages at
sunrise.
Tell me why is it that you hide?
In plain sight,
yet the image is blurred.
Knowing exactly what to say,
yet somehow my speech is slurred.
Love is painted on my brain.
I can't escape the agony.
I just hope you know what you're doing
and soon come rescue me.

Captivism

A layer of my aura is covered in you.
I can't escape your essence.
I felt your kisses through the late-night breeze.
It sent warmth streaming through my door.
Inebriated off of your fumes;
They hold me hostage in every space that I
occupy.
My prison holds no locks or doors,
      just an infinite blanket of you.
This self-submerging of you allowed my
loneliness
      to be subdued.

You were around every corner I turned.
In the eyes of every stranger I met.
I saw you in their walks.
I heard you in their dialects.
They even left trails of you dancing in my
nostrils
      long after they went away.
Some sort of purgatory;
A heavenly hell.
Not sure if I wanted to stay.

I knew I had you when in your sleep,
      your body yearned for me to hold.

It was there that I tantalized and captivated
your soul
True love in spirit.
Somehow the physical went askew.
Both subconsciously running from what our
hearts
      both know is true.
We can recreate our love.
Mold it into what we need it to be like clay.
Let our actions reflect all the words we're both
afraid to say.

Your majestic demeanor tells me that you know
      you're in the presence of a Goddess.
No jewels to represent a status.
Before me you stand genuine and modest.
Beautiful memories carry me on this journey,
      still some elements catch me by
surprise.
Enchanted by your love;
I hope the finish line of this race ends with me
by your side.

Lucid

Your arms are my refuge.
My private utopia.
Your presence alone makes my heart smile.
The thought of your absence brings confusion
much like a
long corridor of echoes;
Loud and discombobulating.
My past brought a love that left me hungry,
and you appeased my appetite.

Serenity

On the gloomiest day you are my sunshine.
You bring a calm that makes troubled waters
still.
Held hostage by my convictions;
You became my liberator
Dubiety reasoning;
You became my elucidator.
You kissed the scars of my past away;
Foolish to think they wouldn't be accepted.

Union

We danced in a field of sunflowers.
Happiness filled our eyes and glistened,
     like drops of morning dew.
Humility streamed down our cheeks as
strength
     seeped through our pores.
Time stopped when our skin met.
Our voices collided.
You were mine and I, yours.
In each other,
     we found all that we had ever wanted
and
        wished for.

Bliss

Your mane is my fortress.
It leaves a scent so sweet.
Your eyes are my solace.
Into a sea of brown sugar,
      I dive deep.
Your stature is like nature;
So crisp and refreshing.
Two souls full of
      LOVE.
What a beautiful
      Blessing.

Solace

Clarity became my therapy,
and in your eyes,
 I found Truth.
The chaotic chatter of my mind,
your voice was there to soothe.
You picked up the broken pieces.
You mended what had ripped.
You took the splinters out of my heart,
and where I needed it,
you stitched.

9

we laid there
nakedly in our garden
like Adam and Eve
on a cool sunny
day

no fruit to be eaten
it was virtuous

with my hair untamed
energy radiating through your pores
you looked me in my eyes and I saw myself
beauty in its purest form

-LOVE-

Inquisition

I'd like to know where your perspective was
before
you went through your shift.
Did you look at the world through scorned shut
eyes?
Were you always programmed for survival?
Unable to give or receive love because it would
crack the boulder
you've placed, for protection, around your
heart.
The pieces would have no choice but to
crumble and slip away,
leaving you bare and vulnerable.
 Did that scare you?

I felt your body shiver as I teased your soul into
ascension.
I provoked it.
Made it feel things that made it crave for more,
but my love,
you resisted.
Knowing evolution was inevitable,
my love for you persisted.

Cognitive Dissonance

My foolish heart.
I wish I could save you from yourself.
Released from captivity,
          though you didn't long to be free.
Like a moth to a flame;
Always had some sort of weird attraction to
pain.
She has a mind of her own you see.
Always going against my wishes.
And in such proximity,
          the inability to see what I could from
afar,
                    left her vulnerable.
Radiating warmth made her conform
          to the grooves in your hand,
                    making her think it was a perfect
          fit.
Your voice was that of a symphony.
With the power to make her run through every
minute
          like life depended.
With the power to make her as still as a broken
clock.
If a heart could do such a thing;
She had jumped down the rabbit hole,
          and didn't stop to think if she should
bring
                    ME!

Heartache

A Hearts Lament

Did your heart tremble?
As you watched the last breath of oxygen leave
my lungs
 and escape my lips,
        did the hair stand up on the back of your
neck?
Tell me;
Did you think twice before you wrapped your
hands
        around my heart?
You caressed and stroked it gently,
        making me fall deeper and deeper into
despair.
Did you hesitate before you ripped her from my
chest?
I Whispered "I love you" as you looked away.
Did you hear me?

We used to dance amongst the clouds.
 You promised me paradise and happy dreams.
Oh how I was deceived.
I stood by watching as you walked away with
my heart.
My skin turned cold.
Eyes dulled with no emotion.

Did you forget that I need that to survive?
Do you even care if I'm alive?
I let you roam further and further away,
        hoping you'd return before frost
encompasses me.

Mirage

I thought I had lost you.
So I testified my love for you to the heavens,
     and begged God to bend his will,
          should your name not be written
in my destiny.

I looked for you,
     in the eyes of strangers,
          but the windows to their souls
were closed.

I looked for you in every set of arms that
embraced me.
Their touch was too cold,
     hands too small,
          shoulders not as broad.

I looked for you in the voices of these strangers,
     but they couldn't compare
          to the smooth sultry notes,
        you send ringing through my
ears.

          No sound. No touch. No
      taste, sight or smell

-dared to be compared to the
authenticity of you.
   And still, I searched.
I was lost.

Spiritually connected, I could feel you all
around me, yet, you were nowhere at all.
You could have warned me it would be this
way. Intoxicated by my tears,
I toast to you while struggling with
this duality of love and hate.
   Still I searched.
Hoping you would meet me at least halfway.

Unaware that you had set me on a shelf.
Your trophy!
Only to be admired from afar,
   -but even you forgot to dust me off from
time to time.

Tainted Pictures

You were everything I never asked for;
And everything I didn't need.
Yet, somehow, I clung to your dysfunction
and loved every bit of it.
I watched you make and break promises to my
heart.
All the while loving and loathing you at the
same time.
Why must you leave your footprints
where I thought my soul existed?
Where I thought mutual love existed?
Was it just sad confusion?
Tell me I'm not the only one living this
delusion.
As long as you're next to me,
I'll stay in the illusion.
Now lately it seems that you're nowhere to be
found.
I run away from the voices of doubt,
but how can I when you're not around?

I loved the idea of love.
I loved the idea of a young lover's tale.
I loved the idea of a picturesque family.
Will you be the hero or the villain?
Is this story a tragedy or a fairytale?

I gave you the key to my heart,
and you went and tried to open the wrong door.
Take the blinders off your eyes.
Can our love be restored?

I love your gentleness.
Though covered in darkness,
it still shined through.
Your delicate gaze into my eyes and protective
demeanor,
made me fall in love with you.
Who cares about materials when we're clothed
in chemistry?
Can we concoct the right reactions?
Will you help me solve this mystery?

I whispered your name to the trees;
They held back all the answers.
So I let the emotions bubble,
and replicate like a cancer
It's getting harder to feel your presence
 Thoughts of good memories get me through
I just hope I don't come to regret
the day I fell in love with you.

The Devil's Workshop

He took something so beautiful;
So majestic.
Something far too precious to ever be
compared to any jewel.
He took something so pure and genuine;
Thought to be irrevocably untarnished, and
crushed it.
What once was a pretty portrait,
now a canvass torn to shreds.
He tainted every image of perfection I ever had.

He brought me so high just to laugh and watch
me fall.
He was a wolf in sheep's clothing.
He illuminated my flaws.
He stripped me of my innocence.
Mind racing;
Overload complete.
He showed me how fear can consume a soul.
He enjoyed my misery.

He showed me things darker than the deepest
depths of the sea.
He showed me a pain that was unbearable.
He was cunning and conniving;
The way he hissed about.

He destroyed my confidence;
Replaced with helplessness and doubt.
He made me dumb, blind, and mute.
I was caught up in his rapture.
Succumbed to his temptations;
My soul unwillingly captured.

He made me question who I was and
everything I aspired to be.
He had me convinced my only outcome was
defeat.
As much as I'd like to hate him,
it was he who helped make me a better person.
At first it was hard to see.
Concession was my only option to get the
turbulence to stop.
But you know what they say,
an idle mind is the

devil's workshop.

Because of You

I found the pieces to the puzzle that you
wanted me to solve.
By the time I found them,
 I didn't know if I could even put them
together.
My heart yearned for you and never could get
close enough.

Your lies made her turn cold.
Your lies made her turn dark.
Your lies made her a sad case of isolation.
Your lies made her anger fester.
You and this cold world made her drown in her
loneliness.
Everything she touched was gold plated.
                    Because of you.
Down,
        Low,
        and sunken into this dark place.

She embraced her shadows;
Though she tried so hard to make them
disappear.
They told her secrets.
They listened.
They helped her escape the loneliness.

They pushed her to embrace herself.
They came perfectly wrapped like presents she
never asked for.
They refused to leave.
                    Because of you.

Her shadows and she became intertwined.
Like lace and corduroy,
they didn't mix,
          but were so beautifully stitched.
                    Because of you.

She had no choice but to stand in her loud
serenity.
She had no choice but to mingle with her
demons;
Who broke her and helped build her up
                    Because of you.

Questions

The world tried to turn me against you,
        -and that made me dive deeper into
your soul.
To ask some more questions like,
        "Why is it you that has my heart in a
hold?"
        "Should I move on?"
        "Could I do it if I tried?"
        "Why could we never share the mutual
feelings
        we have inside?"
I was afraid of vulnerability.
What was it that you were trying to hide?

Death in Retrospect

Death was by far my hardest lesson.
Somehow we never really got acquainted.
I experienced it vicariously through others.
I even felt the throngs of its pains.
We were disassociated until I was faced with
Truth.
Truth can bring blows so tumultuous,
It'll have you begging for death to take you.
Maybe there,
       behind the veil
I can finally have my peace.

My truth was from a lover who showed me
things
I wasn't ready to see.
He was a man,
who stood before me in all his splendor.
Now, a boy draped in rags.
A light that once shined bright;
Brought down to just a glimmer.

I must have mourned his death at least a
million times;
Yet, he was only a phone call away.
A phone call that would plague him with my
ugly sorrows;

If only I could muster up the courage to say. All the
things that left me broken.

All the things that fueled a fire that left me
scorched alive.

All the things that left me hunched over in
agony, unable to control the liquid hurt
streaming from my eyes.

All the misery he brought,
meant to teach unconditional love.
Meant to identify emotional attachments that
God was trying to strip me of.

This lesson became too overwhelming.
I couldn't comprehend or grasp it.
Why does my lover have to die in my eyes?
                              Yet,
still, for him, I hold so much passion
My heart is filled with love,
but this wall I built is numbing.
Just waiting for the day I heal and this pain
becomes redundant.

3D Delusions

I stayed up all night blotting tears from my
pillow
-and trying to get the pieces of my heart off the
rug.
Every piece represented all of our issues;
There were just too many to pick them up.
So I left them on the floor.
Walked away with my heart sore.

You couldn't look me in the eyes
-the last time we encountered.
Your demeanor spoke to my spirit;
I could tell you were feeling somber.
Did you sense it in my touch?
Or hear it in my voice?
Thoughts of coming to our conclusion;
It seems you've left me no other choice.

You see,
 your inability to love opened my eyes
-to things that were never seen.
I fell in love with your potential;
Not knowing if you could ever be.
However,
        transformation is inescapable.
Just waiting on divine time,

-but my patience is wearing thin.
Unsure if I can keep standing by.

See you got with me when I was broken.
Grew quickly attached to your affections.
Then slowly you withdrew.
Should have known by your inflections,
-of the way you used to hold me.
I saw the twinkle in your eyes,
-but it was covered in so much guilt;
Already knew the secrets you tried to hide.

Can you tell me what you feelin'?
Did you ever have a plan for us?
Why keep me hidden as a trophy?
Were you intimidated by love?
Why do you think that you're not worthy?
Why do you try to hide your light?

I see you and see strength.
I see you and see something divine.

Could I have broken down those walls?
Could I have given more support?

Wanted to encompass you in love,
-but your reception was unsure.
There's no denying our connection.
Telepathically your messages come through.
Fifth dimension fairytales.
Just need them in the 3D to come true.

You are a knight in shining armor.
You are a midsummer's night dream.
I'm Rapunzel waiting in her tower.
Won't you come and save your queen?
Let's run away from the superficial.
Let's join together and find peace.
Let's embrace our spirituality.
Explore places we've never seen.

Get off that rollercoaster.
I can see you're not happy with your life.
Won't find that place of true tranquility,
-til you have me by your side.

I tried to lead you to the water.
I left a trail of light in my wake.
You kept clinging to dysfunction,
-so my gifts you didn't take.

Don't you let this cold world blind you.
Don't deny yourself this warmth.
Don't let this world full of false delusions get
you to conform.
You have the power in your hands.
Just tell me what we both know your heart
yearns.
Step out on faith.
Embrace the change.
Accept love.
Reject the hurt.

I'm always in your corner.
The road to bliss,
-we have the keys.
Will you leave me hanging on this journey?
Decision time
To stay.
Or leave.

Healing & Acceptance

Dark Night of the Soul

It was painful. Those nights I spent alone. So I turned to the voices for comfort when even the noise of the world wasn't enough to drown out my loneliness. Demons I thought I slew reiterated our acquaintances. Intrigued by Pandora's Box, no consequences were weighed. They led me on a chase. I couldn't reach the finish line. I tripped, stumbled and fell over all the disappointments they laid at my feet. Down into an abyss of fire, I ran from echoes. I chased memories that never happened. I saw blue and purple flames, then darkness. I watched the eyes of souls turn vacant as they cast screams that would never be heard over this blanket of infinite void. I pushed and shoved my way through chaos, longing for the familiarity of my cell. Questing for my captor; Both hero and villain. The screams turned to whispers. Incubus met me in my chambers. I couldn't getaway. Menses of my eyes left specks of guilt smudged within my sheets. I awakened, in the rainforest. Kindred spirits were all around me. I began to walk mile after mile. I felt pieces of myself crack and slip away. I never looked back. Hummingbirds kissed my cheeks. I watched the sun rise to meet the moon. I danced amongst the colors; Hues of pinks, blues, and yellows. I met a white owl, whose name is Phillipe. His gentle stare sent warmth through every extremity. I was home. Alas! I let my ego slip too far past my reach to grasp and I stretched my hands toward the Sun.

Transcendence

A cloak of despair encompasses me as I sit in
separation of you.
Two thrones,
        faced in opposite directions.
Only I ruled alone because you didn't want to
pick up your crown.
You didn't think you were worthy.
You didn't think love was allowed.
So I sat back and watched you wander.
Didn't want you to feel rushed,
even though I was willing to accept the aspects
of yourself
        that make you want to blush.
You know the pieces you try to hide from the
world,
when you're alone,
        looking in the mirror
The shadows you try to confront before you
bring them into a relationship
        for someone else to bear.

Just bring me all those flaws.
Watch me transform them into power.

Let me show you a love so divine,
everyone will want to emulate ours.
Let me bring you into transcendence.
Pick a point and let's begin.
Let me cover you in this light.
Turn you over to God to make amends.
He sends me visions of you in my sleep.
It's up to you to ascend.
I felt your soul collapse in my arms,
but your body remained tense.
Your vulnerability is inevitable.
What are you waiting for?
Let me in.
A God intimidated by a Goddess?
We both hold divinity within.

Yin and Yang

He grinds his teeth.
Through the cool breeze brought by a warm
summers night,
I heard him.
Grinding out his troubles.
Grinding out his pains.
I wanted to shield him from his trials;
Only I knew it would stunt his growth.
I wanted to be his rehabilitation;
Only the separation between us was so great,
I could feel it even in his presence.
I realized that we both couldn't accept affection
        without thoughts of apprehension
                    flashing
            through our minds.
I realized that I was his mirror and he was
mine.
All of my self-doubt and lack of confidence,
        he brought to the surface.
I was his light.
He was my darkness.
One soul split in two with one purpose.
He laid out all of the problems of my past.

Helped me confront generational curses,
       and I began to heal.
Had to stop running from those painful
memories
       and emotions that were necessary to
feel.
Needed for the growth and evolution of us as a
collective.
He was the catalyst on a journey to combat all
of my transgressions.
Warriors of love.
Though sometimes the battle felt strenuous
and left us timid.
A disguised blessing from up above,
meant for our ascension.

Afflicting Acceptance

We became enmeshed and I felt you in me.
Felt you in my heart.
Felt you in my soul.
I became entangled in all of your pain and
chaos.
I soaked up your faults and flaws;
They became my own.
What a journey they plundered me upon.
Only my hell was in a different perspective.
My hell was played over and over in my
thoughts and dreams.
I couldn't escape it.
I felt generations of wounded men.
A progeny of mixed emotions.
My hell made me question if the hell I was
living in
 was better than the hell I would return to in
my slumber.
A soul in captivity;
Though the attainment of freedom was never
desired.
I took those emotions and examined them.
I picked each one apart.

I spoke to them.
Sometimes the conversations became intense.
I began to intermingle and intertwine.
I was able to soothe them.
Make all negativity dissipate from my essence.
Within me,
 I brought them to peace.

Infinite Love

My love can't fit in a specific paradigm;
For the love I have for you can't be
comprehended in this dimension.
I admire your perseverance;
I admire your ambition.
I've endured every pain you've experienced;
Just in a different way.
I knew the secrets you tried to hide from me
before you could say.
I've felt the hollowness you've harbored.
I've gone through the struggles you've tried to
forget.
I tried to let you go,
        but you still inhabit spaces in my
consciousness that I can't seem to clear.
You represent everything that's imperfectly
perfect to me.
To some it's strictly chaos.
For me,
        so simply complex.
I loved you before I knew you.
It was written in the stars;

Though you introduced me to shadows within
myself that I didn't know existed.

Loving you catalyzed my evolution.
Catalyzed a revolution of self.
Love was the water I never knew I thirsted for.
You saw the seed,
watered it,
        sat back and watched it grow.
You made a rose bloom out of the mud.
You true contribution to transformation,
I don't think you'll ever know.
Drew me closer to God.
Who in turn molded me into a
                Goddess.
Helped me strip the aspects of myself that I'm
not too proud of.

Can't seem to shake you.
Just want to thank you,
for all the lessons you've bestowed.
I found the stars to my moon.
Yin to my yang.
Reflection to my soul.
Connection so divine,
but as individuals we have to grow.
And until it's perfectly aligned,
I have to let you go.

Metamorphosis

Just a lamb appeased by milk.
The rubies of this world are infinitesimal to the
jewels that await in a different dimension.
Still, I conformed to what society wanted me to
be.
A superficial figment of another's imagination.
Pulling and clipping my cords;
Only to bring me closer to obliteration.

Self-digestion both obligatory and imminent.
I encased my shadows and withdrew from the
world.
Heavily medicated,
I slipped into a meditative state.
Dressed in white linen,
I stripped myself.
A virgin.
I was clean.

Rehab

How do you rehabilitate a wounded Goddess?
Is she exiled from her throne?
Do you throw her into isolation until the pain is
overthrown?
Can she make sound judgments?
Is it wise for her to rule?
How do you create warmth within her heart
when it turns cold?
What do you do?
A flower only partly bloomed,
dying to emerge and eat the fruits of life.
She envisions love;
Encapsulation of balance and harmony.
On a quest to rid herself of strife.
How do you rehabilitate a wounded Goddess?
You cover her in cloth;
Not the kind that can be felt in the mundane.
You cover her in cloth of love to subside all the
pain
Cover her in warmth.
Create an environment of serenity.
Where the trees can whisper secrets,
and the birds can sing their bliss.
This is how you rehabilitate a wounded
Goddess
when her soul has gone amiss.

Reconciliation with Self

There was a war within me.
A well of void so deep, sometimes I thought I'd drown.
I had taken on the responsibility of all the generational curses that permeated my lineage.
A journey so intrinsic;
I couldn't escape its wrath.
I could feel my heart sink deeper in my chest with every bout of sorrow that was thrown in my path.
To hide my scars,
every bout,
        the outcome of me became more luminescent.
Every trail of pain-stricken tears
only led to the reconstruction of me.
I battled abuse, addictions and self-doubt.
I challenged my constrictions.
I used Love as a way out.
Introduced to my shadows.
Apart of me and I of thee.
Even in my peace,
I realized that they would never leave.
For what's the beauty of blue skies
if you've never seen the grays?
What's joy if you've never experienced pain?

My shadows swallowed me in darkness.
At times I couldn't see the light.
They initiated an uncomfortable feeling so
great,
but it was there that I thrived.

Ascension

She was strong;
But not because she wanted to be.
She was strong because she had to be.
She developed a skin so thick,
she could walk on hot coal and come out
unscathed.
She was a million-piece puzzle;
So well put together.
She had her pieces glued and mounted.
She was untouchable,
but she wasn't egocentric.
One might wonder if they were worthy of her
presence;
 The way she flourished in immanence.
She was peace.
With a touch of humility that was too genuine
to be forced or faked.
She was the embodiment of sensuality.
She was sun-kissed.
A kaleidoscopic dream.
She left you craving for her presence,
even in your sleep.
She was the missing key that belonged to a lock
that had become rusted,
but held so many secret wonders of love and
abundance.

She was a prowess.
 A sensationalist.
A diamond.
Look at her shine.
She was a luminary.
She brought heat to a cold world
filled with hate and violent crimes.
All her battles were preparation.
It seemed God gave her the hardest.
They made her step into her strength,
as she was molded into a
       GODDESS.

Transformation

Voices

Trepidation slid
        slowly
past my shoulders and
        down
to my knees.
Fear swam in my belly.
Why do they insist on provoking me?
The voices sent me through the underworld.
Tried to run,
but couldn't leave.
Mind stretched in different directions—
Will someone come rescue me?

They told me to embrace my failures.
They told me to give up on my dreams.
I tried to run for cover,
and no one heard my screams.

The universe sent me synchronicities
that brought up old wounds.
Things I thought I had healed,
but I had spoken too soon.

I had to sit with my insecurities.
I had to re-examine my flaws.
I had to challenge my beliefs.

I had to accept the things within this world
that others couldn't see.

I was sent through the fire.
Went in as soft as clay.
I had to get comfortable with the voices.
After a while,
I wanted them to stay.

They made me accept my shadows.
They helped me transform my weaknesses
into strengths.
They helped push forward,
when all I wanted to do was give in.

"Forces"

Why are there forces in this world that don't
want me to shine?
That want to dim my light that will always
shine bright?
Through the clouds.
Through the rain.
Through the strongest winds of winters night.
Sending wiles and tricks my way;
Demons that attack my mind.

Why are there forces in this world afraid of my
power?
Envy and hate sending curses,
that can never knock me off my throne.
They try to tell me I'm not worthy.
They say I'm here in this world alone.

I bind these forces.
Combat them with love.
When their transgressions get too heavy,
I conjure the light.
I make them chew on their spite as I pass
through my rites.
An uphill and losing battle for the opposition.
Whose hurdles only prepare me for my divine
mission.

Did they think that I would fall?
Shot by those toils they call bullets.
Or that I would shiver away in fear?
I come from a lineage of strong black women.
It's in my genes to irrupt through barriers,
swallow, and conquer fears.

Do they not know who they're messing with?
A **Goddess**,
molded by God's own hands.
My armor can't be penetrated.
When knocked down,
I get back up and stand.

I trudged through snares.
I broke the chains that were meant to hold me
back.
Turned my imperfections into strengths;
Laced my disposition with poise and tact.

You see the characteristics of my mind are rich
in originality,
and can't be tainted.
These superficial constructs and standards of
society
won't disorganize or rearrange it.

They can try to take my throne.
Try to take my crown,
but they'll never be able to fit it.

Try to take my spot,
but can't walk my walk.
They gotta' try harder to get it.

Waves

The waves rolled
I was anxious
The waves calmed
I was soothed
The waved retracted
I was lonely
The waves enthralled
I was loved
The waves collapsed
I was broken
The waves built
I was confident
The waves destroyed
I was hurt
The waves replenished
I was joyful
All in all,
when it's all said,
what the waves did is what my soul reflects

Out of the Abyss

What do you call a house with no walls?
A house with no doors?
What do you call a place with no memories?
Is it a home?
How can we unlock the chest that holds too
many secrets?
Secrets of sorrow and mourning—
Secrets of loneliness and longing—
Shadows creep in and whisper to my
insecurities.
Though the blinds are shut,
      somehow,
 I still search for the light.
Knowing all along the light is in the mirror.
A mere reflection of my shadows.
Without them I cannot thrive.
A seesaw of emotions.
I almost drown trying to stay alive.
I whispered back to those dark voices.
I cast illumination on my doubts.
I replaced my fears with stability.
Finally, I am free

God's Daughter

I sprinkled glitter on my wounds,
 and watched them manifest into medals.
I brushed my thoughts with an air of positivity,
 and they metamorphosed into peace.
I pushed through barriers that were meant to
contain me,
 and never held a grudge.
I kept my feet planted when the stormy winds
came
and I didn't budge.
I rejoiced.
I sang a song to the heavens,
and laid my problems at God's feet.
I heard the sweetest song when he or she
welcomed,
and answered me.
I jumped through hoops.
I ran through fire.
I saw the gates of hell.
Cognitive dissonance—
Two dimensions—
Who's who—
What's what—

It's hard to tell.
Through it all I kept my faith.
I couldn't let it falter.
I'm covered in the light.
I'll always be God's daughter.

Magic

I danced amongst the moon and stars.
I sprinkled sunshine with my smile.
I brought warmth to the coldest settings.
I watched doves fly over the horizon.
A beautiful rose that doesn't wither.
A beautiful song that never ends.
A beautiful bird with the prettiest voice.
I sucked the darkness out of every corner that
held no light.
I oozed magnificence within the clouds.
I created magic with my heart and eyes.

Reflections

Through reflection,
I learned my greatest lessons.
I dove into the core of my essence
through rigorous sessions of introspection.
I got well acquainted with my pain.
Stitched old wounds shut,
so my peace would be gained.

 I was introduced to the roots of my anger.
Absorbed the residue of nasty emotions;
Left them hanging in my closet like
unnecessary hangers.

I battled my inner voice.
To love or hate myself?
I had to make that choice.

All too often,
I found that self was hard to conquer.
I grasped for light in a world so dark,
to prevent the making of a monster.

Then I looked into the mirror.

Spoke to all my flaws—
Shook all my demons—
      To me,
it all became much clearer.

My pain, anger, insecurities, and
transgressions
were meant to make me stronger.
I was knocked down,
But my faith picked me up
when I thought I couldn't take it any longer.
In the depths of my sorrows,
I caught a glimmer of the light.
I kept my feet planted on my journey,
when it seemed,
the road ahead,
I had lost
            Sight.

Morning Song

Little blackbird,
won't you sing your morning song?
Take me to a place with sunny blue skies
Where I can hear raindrops falling on tin.

Little blackbird,
won't you sing your morning song?
Take me to the rainforest,
so that I can commune with the plants
and thank mother nature for all of her nectar.

Please, little blackbird,
won't you sing your morning song?
Take me to where Oshun can bless me with her
rays of beauty,
and Yemaya can soothe me with her waters.

Little blackbird,
won't you sing your morning song?
Take me to a place where I can feel the strength
of Chango course through my vessel,
as I pound drums to release my rage.

Little blackbird,

won't you sing your morning song?
Take me to a place where I'm surrounded by
white owls,
while I soak up wisdom from Obatala.

Little blackbird,
won't you sing your morning song?
Take me to a beautiful patch in the wilderness,
where Ogun offers his blanket of protection.
Won't you sing your morning song,
little blackbird?
Take me to a field of lilies,
where I can mumble all of my problems,
and Elegua offers me his ear.
Where I can embody the warrioress energy of
Oya,
to combat and conquer all my fears.

Oh, little blackbird,
won't you please come and sing your morning
song?

Progression of the Heart

I had hope in the slightest glint of sun,
      through the thickest billow of clouds.
When the chaos of the world almost completely
consumed me,
      LOVE came in and led me out.
This was how I was introduced to the new me.

A soul with much grace.
With intelligence to match.
Whose beam shined so bright it reflected the
luminescence
      of the brightest star.
A rose that can bloom in December;
Or like a skeleton flower in the rain,
      my beauty was translucent.
It covered the scars of all my pain.

I began to love deeply.
I grew closer to Mother Earth.
I began to respect all life.
Began to feel when others hurt.

In me, the desire to make a difference grew.
A desire to take back our communities.
Be a positive example for our youth.
I wanted to show others the power of
unconditional love.
Wanted to create a sense of unity and pick
others up.

Hold a sense of accountability and raise
vibrations.
Begin to heal the residual grief of past
generations.

Who knew the trials I'd have to face?
The demons I'd have to battle?
Who knew the traumas I'd have to revisit and
heal from?
I had to.

Sometimes the past holds scars that keep up
chained.
It's time to break free.
Take back control of mind, body and soul.
Open eyes to things we never knew could be.

Before: just a wanderer
Light spirit.
Unknown purpose.
Now: a sunflower in its bloom
Beautiful heart.

Ethereal presence.
Forgiving and nurturing.

The sun lent me its beauty.
I got my poise from the moon.
I danced and shimmed with dualities as I
became attuned.
From the loins of disgrace,
a fallen Goddess now renewed.
On a quest to fulfill my purpose and to myself
stay true.

Answer

My wounds became scars that were almost
impossible to see.
My trials: a distant memory.
Life was my teacher.
All my lessons, I passed the tests.
Standing tall.
Standing strong.
I had to give my best.
My faith was the saddle that rode me through
the pasture,
         of life's unexpected events and natural
disasters.
Wishing that relief would come just a little bit
faster.
I was led to the water and God showed me love.
All my transgressions were behind me.
In Love,
         I was lifted up.
Covered in armor of strength.
Covered in a blanket of protection.
To find truth within myself,
         Love was the answer to all my questions.

Phoenix Rising

I wonder how many people heard my cries.
How many listened to me sing songs to the
moon.
How many watched me dance beneath the
stars.
Did I send too many wishes flying across the
sky
      too soon?

Smoke rose.
Through the clouds, I could see myself running
further
      away from the sobriety of my addictive
behaviors.
Down into a spiral of mixed emotions,
      grasping for my dreams.
I swam against currents of fear and rejection,
 unable to get relief,
         or so
it seemed.

Pain was present.
Beneath my eyelids,
      there was no well.
Silent screams from my mental hell,
      and there was no one that I could tell.

A blessing in disguise.
A phoenix rising from the ashes.
All my turmoil became my teacher.
All my grief pushed me towards my passions.
Balancing light and dark and having to go
    within.
Absorb all of my imperfections and turn them
into strengths.
To conquer all my demons,
    I spoke them all away.
Forced into hibernation,
    but now I'm wide awake.

Revolution

Hibernation

Flames of bright red and orange
  rose before the gates of
    Oppression.
High pitched crooning and crackling.
Flames of cool blues and purples
  rose before the gates of injustice.
Low rumbling that turns into a growl.
Bloodily beaten and bruised.
Layers stripped like a sweet onion.
Seeds planted under rubble;
Never meant to grow.
Seeds scattered in the wilderness;
Domestication, they'll never know.
Glimpses of a revolution lurk just beyond the
horizon.
The Sun.
The Stars.
The Moon
    meet.
The wicked become fearful.
They despise it.
For the wicked know no rage
    -like those who've been oppressed.
They can't fathom the tears of struggle

-from those who give their best.
Left with the
      c r u m b s
-that society paints as acceptable.
Unaware of a Grand Demise.
The monsters rage has been caressed.
What will they do when it decides to
      RISE?

Why

Why must you poke and prod a monster
-that doesn't want to be awakened?
Why must you try to unlock doors covered in
cement?
Why must you pluck the petals of a lily
-that sways uninhibited in a field?
Why must you cover the sun with your clouds?
Why must you pull the strings
-that don't want to be tugged?
Why must you shape the clay
-that doesn't want to be molded?
Why must you peel the scab
-that hasn't healed?
Why must you search for things
-that don't want to be found?
Why must you feed the mouth
-that doesn't want to be fed?
                    Why?

Take Me Back

Take me back to the ancient pyramids;
To the time when dynasties were ruled by
Ma'at.
Take me back to the times of Cleopatra.
Take me back to my
   Royal
     Roots;
A time before the
  entrapment
of my ancestors.
A time before Harriet Tubman and Sojourner
Truth.
   A time before Rosa Parks.
Take me back to the time of the
   Moors.
A times where my melanated skin equated to
     POWER.
Take me back to a time when we were teachers
and scholars.
Can someone please take me back?
A time when bronze kissed skin was beautiful
  -and we lived like the royal Kings and
Queens
     we were born to be.
     Take me back.

Visions

Let's join hands and build a fortress.
Let the mountains voice their rage to the
heavens.
Let the trees sway their limbs in the late-night
breeze;
as they give the solutions to the puzzles
        -that have yet to be solved.
Nations have fallen.
Men will attempt to rise.
The way of the wicked cannot prevail.
You can see it in their eyes.
Can you smell the fear?
Can you hear their hearts tremble?
They try to sequester their motives,
but for their greed,
there is no thimble.
        Let's go back to a time of peace.
When respect for all species rang true.
        Let's go back to a time of unity.
When you didn't have to worry about if anyone
would judge you.
Take us back to the origin.
        Let's take back our indigenous roots.
Just looking for

Peace
         Equality
                and Reparations.
Just looking for a solution to stop all this
separation.
The constellations,
        -they tell a story.
You can map it with the moon.
I keep dreaming of a resurrection.
It's written in the stars and its coming soon.

Tear Drops Full

My teardrops are filled
　　　with the hunger of the children in Syria.
My teardrops are filled
　　　with the pain of men who can't feed
their families in Africa.
My teardrops are filled
　　　with devastating bombs that are
dropped every day,
　　　-by wicked men on their quest for
Power.
My teardrops are filled
　　　with the hate that black men cast on
　　　-their beautiful black Queens.
My teardrops are filled
　　　with the agony of young girls,
　　　-who never had a positive role model.
My teardrops are filled
　　　with the devastation of women,
　　　- who solicit their bodies to perverted
men to make ends meet.
My teardrops are filled
　　　with the heartache of women,
　　　-who were never taught how they should
be treated.
My teardrops are filled
　　　with the void of these women,

-who never grew up with a father.
My teardrops are filled
        With empathy for men that have been
castrated by society.
My teardrops are filled
        with the anger of men who have been
ripped away from their families
        -by an unjust justice system.
My teardrops are filled
        with traumas that need to be addressed.
My teardrops are Full.

What is Freedom

What is war in the eyes of the oppressed?
-A systematic machine of lies-
We encounter war every day.
-Hip to the deceit they try to hide-
We demand justice
 and get a superficial appeasement of our
needs.
They cloak their shams under the illusion
that we live in the land of the free.
 What really is freedom to a mind that's been
                            -enslaved-
          What is freedom to one who gets their
hands dirty
                    and bend over backward,
just to eat each day?
          What is freedom to those who've been
taught
                    to live in competition?
At war with their own people.
Within the communities,
          there's sedition.
          What is freedom to a child who doesn't
know their roots?
To the teenager that's subject to a corrupt
justice system

that tells him to put his hands up before
they shoot.
What is freedom to the mother that has
to work three jobs?
To the man who gets out of prison and labeled
a felon
now for the rest of his life,
mentally he's scarred.
What is Freedom and how can
one attain it?
Do we dissimulate a dirty past,
that our DNA is all stained with?
Is there hope for a future with equality?
Will we ever know peace?
What is Freedom to people,
who don't even make up their own
beliefs?

Cycle

They say there's poison in the food,
so what do we eat?
Went vegan,
but now there's poison in the vegetables.
Might as well eat meat.

They say there's poison in the air,
so how do we breathe?
Might as well keep smoking these cigarettes
        that's slowly killing me.

 I went to the corner store
to get some food in my belly.
All they had to offer was fried chicken,
cheeseburgers and watermelon.
That's okay cuz I can get it with the EBT.
Maybe if mamas not too tired when she gets off
work
she can cook for me.
Mama came home fussin' bout some dishes in
the sink,
so I took off with my friends.
Gave her some time to think.
The street lights came on and I didn't make it
home.
I left the house in a hurry,

now mama cant reach me on the phone
-and I still ain't get no dinner so my stomach is
on groan.
I stopped by the corner store
to get some food in my belly.
All they had to offer was fried chicken,
cheeseburgers and watermelon.
That's okay cuz I can get it with the EBT.
Got home;
no food in the kitchen cuz mama went to sleep.

Make a Change

Chase the light and make a change.
See the diamonds in your children's eyes.
Choose benevolence.
Stop the hate.
Give a stranger a hug.
Put down the weapons.
No pointing fingers.
Let the homeless find shelter.
Blind your eyes to color and unite.
Faith.
Love.
Peace.
Happiness.
Love will always prevail.
Vanquish hate, greed and envy.

Death to Willie Lynch

400 years of bondage.
We have yet to see the reparations.
Baby momma trippin',
daddy gotta go.
They infiltrate through separation.

400 years of whips and chains
they drug across our backs.
Stand in line for them new Jays.
Rob,
      Steal,
            Kill each other.
They sit back and laugh.

400 years of struggle.
Drinking out those dirty gourds.
Brothers and sisters,
150 years later;
They still take everything we worked for.

On the banks of James river,
we let the seal our fate.
Virginia.
1712.
Not sure the month or day.

400 years of mistreatment
caused us to become animalistic.
They call us monkeys.
Give us guns,
and hope we all become statistics.

400 years of sorrow.
They ostracized our men.
Now our women don't respect them
cuz they all
                    Independent.

400 years of lies.
Light skin.
Dark skin.
Red or yellow.
They instilled fear, distrust, and envy,
then threw us all into these ghettos.

No money for our infrastructures,
when different nations get relief.
Eulogizing our ignorance,
plotting our demise,
but we can't see.

400 years.
They looked at us with deprecation.
It's true that fear is stronger than love
and envy stronger than adulation.
Now our youth look up to drug dealers,
who disparage education.

What happened to the O.G's that really
gave a fuck?
Excuse my language,
but these new O.G's are misguided.
They're quick to give a gun.
Stray bullets flying through our
communities.
Mothers losing their sons.

400 years of bondage taught us to be
ashamed of our skin.
They demonized our symbols,
but 6 protons, neutrons, and electrons
is what makes up
                    MELANIN.

400 years.
Can we remember what they did to the
Moors?
I'm giving too much too soon.
I can't say no more.

My people!
We need to RISE!
In due time you'll see a resurrection.
I'm just a messenger looking for peace,
                    but its time for

Insurrection.

About the Author

Domonique Tirah Smith is an author and poet who lives in Rochester, New York with her 6-year-old son, 8-month-old daughter, and her companionable Pitbull.

A Navy veteran, Domonique got her start in spoken word poetry, shortly after being honorably discharged. Her spiritual questing and her writing have helped her not only recover from heartache, but also combat P.T.S.D with strength and resilience. She's been writing since her early adolescent years and hopes to use her platform to bring about self-reflection and peace within individuals. She also hopes to embody and help shape reformation within black communities. She believes that can be achieved by using unity to demand the changes we wish to see.